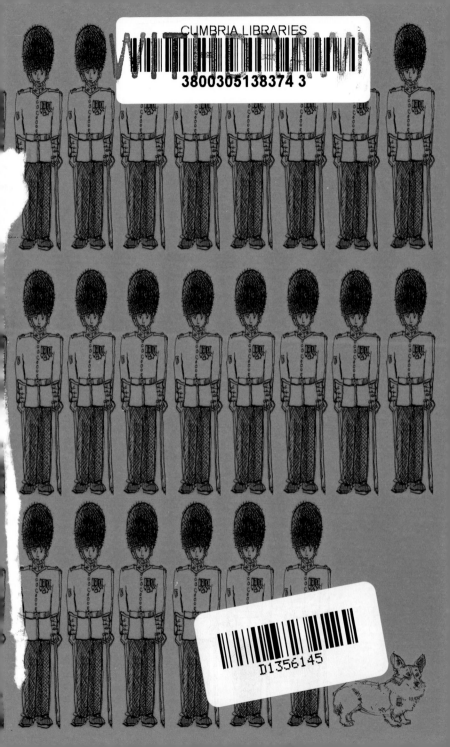

Where's Ma'am?

About the Author

Muick was born in Wales and joined the
Royal Family early in 2021. He splits his time
between London and Scotland.

Illustrated by Madeleine Floyd
Text by Muick with assistance from Helen Coyle

Where's Ma'am?
by
MUICK
The Queen's Corgi

Bedford
Square
PUBLISHERS

First published in 2022 by
Bedford Square Publishers

10 9 8 7 6 5 4 3 2 1

Text © 2022 Helen Coyle
Illustrations © 2022 Madeleine Floyd

British Library Cataloguing-in-Publication Data
A catalogue record for this book is available on request
from the British Library.

ISBN: 978-1-915798-00-8

Designed and typeset by Karen Lilje
Project management by whitefox
Printed and bound in Suffolk by Clays, Ltd, Elcograf S.p.A.

Bedford Square Publishers Ltd
14 Bedford Square
London WC1B 3JA

www.bedfordsquarepublishers.co.uk

WHERE'S MASTER?
by CAESAR, The King's Dog

This book is inspired by the 1910 publication *Where's Master?*, which was narrated by King Edward VII's dog Caesar. Caesar was a wire-haired fox terrier who became the King's favourite and accompanied him everywhere, often travelling abroad to France and Germany. At the King's funeral Caesar processed behind the coffin, and he came to represent a nation's grief at losing its popular monarch.

Where's Master? was published soon after the King's death, and immediately became a bestseller, reprinting fifteen times before the end of the year. The book was published by Hodder & Stoughton with only Caesar as the named author. It was written by the publisher Ernest Hodder-Williams, who was at first summoned to the palace and asked to reveal his sources but later congratulated for creating a sentimental story that reflected the emotions of millions.

Balmoral Castle

Where is she? I've been looking for ages now and I can't find her anywhere. She's not reading in the library, she's not sitting at her desk or resting on the squishy green sofa that we share in the afternoons when we're both tired. I've been out to the boot room with the boots and coats and up the winding stairs to the top of the tower. I've been into the grand mirrored ballroom with the tall windows and the glittering chandeliers and the slippery floor that makes my feet slide out from underneath me when I run. I've been everywhere I can think of. No trace of her anywhere.

Wait a minute. Maybe she's in the garden, sitting on that marvellous bench that was made especially for her? I'll go and have a look . . . Perhaps she's watching the sun set over Mount Lochnagar. She seems to like it there. She sits peacefully for ever such a long time. When I flop down next to her she scratches my head gently and says, 'Now that's what I call a view, Muick. That's a view to be proud of.'

Off I go, down the wide wooden staircase, through the hall, past the cold stone statue that gave me a fright the first time I came to the castle, and then along the corridor and through the heavy felt-covered swing doors into the room with the rows of wellington boots that smell of wet grass and freshly turned mud. There's a whiff of something very interesting and I really want to stop and investigate but I don't, because I must find her.

It's getting dark out there and the people don't seem to like her sitting outside in the evening any more. They're getting very fussy, all the people. They keep shushing me out of the way and telling me not to get under HRH's feet.

Round this corner I go and . . . Oh. Here's the bench but there's no sign of her. I snuffle about a bit. Not a trace of her scent; nothing at all.

I don't understand where she is. If she's had to go away on a trip, why hasn't she taken me with her? I go everywhere with her usually. I miss her voice and her laugh. I miss her kind hands that know exactly how to play with my ears and tickle my chin.

Where is she? Where's Ma'am?

When I woke up this afternoon I was feeling a bit peckish. So I scrambled out of my basket and was just heading towards the kitchens to see if there were any snacks going, when I heard voices coming from her bedroom. She is very rarely in there during the day so I didn't hold out much hope, but I thought I should go and make sure.

When I got to the door of her room, it was closed. I heard someone with a deep voice talking, on and on, and then finally I heard her. She sounded very quiet. I'd found her! I gave a little bark to let her know I was there, but nobody came to

4

open the door. That was odd. Everyone knows that I am to be let in because she is always pleased to see me.

Her voice sounded tired. I wanted so badly to be with her but nobody was paying me any attention, which made me cross. So I started to whine a little. That usually works.

Just then, one of the people came by. It was one of the ones who wear long red coats and black trousers with a sharp fold down the middle of each leg. They take it in turns to let Sandy and me out for our first walk in the morning, and they feed us our breakfast. They're often a bit grumpy at that time of the day, poor things, but generally we all get along pretty well. Ma'am used to take us for our proper walk in the afternoon, although that hasn't happened so much lately.

When I saw this red-coat person, I recognised him immediately. So I stopped whining and gave a little bark to let him know I needed to be let in. If I could only curl up with her, I knew I could make her feel less tired. But today the red-coat man wasn't at all like his normal self. He didn't tickle my ears, he just shooed me away.

So I hid behind a half-open door and waited for him to hurry on elsewhere.

Then I came back and scratched at her bedroom door. I scratched so much that my claw pulled a big flake of paint away. I shall be in trouble for that. Not that *she* ever minds about these things, but some of the other people do.

Just as I was about to give up and howl to get her attention, her door flew open and two people came out. I darted between their legs and one of them muttered something about 'damn dogs' and then I was there; right up standing beside her bedside, reporting for duty and waiting for her to pat the eiderdown beside her, which is her way of giving me permission to jump up and join her. I snuggled down and tucked my head under her hand.

It worked like a charm. She started to smile, stroking my head and waving her other hand at the person in the white coat and the person in the long red coat. They quietly left the room.

That was good. Much better. She and I were together again, and I was so happy. I curled up with my back pressed into her side.

I was falling asleep but she wanted to talk so I tried to stay awake and listen.

She likes to chat when it's just the two of us. When I was a tiny puppy she took me for walks every afternoon in the park. I always knew when we were going out together because I would spot her tying the knot of a headscarf under her chin as she called to Sandy and me. There were never any walkies when she had one of those heavy jewelled things on her head, nor when she was wearing one of those brightly coloured stiff hats with decorations on them, but if she put on a soft silky scarf then we would start to jump around at her feet because we knew that we were all going out together. The best of times.

She hasn't taken me on many walks since we got here. Sandy misses her too, but not as much as I do.

This morning I woke up feeling very out of sorts. I'd been having nightmares about dead pheasants and getting lost on the grouse moors, and not even a hearty breakfast of venison sausages was enough to cheer me up.

When I went outside to stretch my legs, I asked Sandy whether she'd noticed anything different about Ma'am lately.

'What sort of different?' asked Sandy, but she didn't stay still long enough for me to answer. She was off chasing butterflies through the flowerbeds and I had to hurry to catch up with her.

'She doesn't take us for walks any more,' I began. 'And I don't hear her laughing as much as I used to.'

Sandy was too busy chasing her tail round and round in circles to answer.

She's a decent enough dog but she's still a bit of a baby. She only arrived here last summer and Ma'am has told me I have to be patient with her.

'The thing is, when Candy the dorgi was poorly, she got very tired,' I continued. 'You were too little to remember. This was just before she left, for the last time.'

That got Sandy's attention. We stared at one another. Was Ma'am going to leave us?

Sandy scampered over and licked my face. Then a dragonfly flew past, just an inch from our noses. Sandy snapped at it and ran off to play.

Something was wrong, I was sure of it, and there was only one person who could make me feel better.

I hurried back indoors. Breakfast would be served by now, which made my mouth water at the thought of the hot buttered toast that might be passed to me under the table. Sure enough, there was a whiff of kippers inviting me up the stairs. It suddenly seemed like a very long time since my first breakfast.

I hurried through the main hallway, beneath the frowning antlered heads that stared down at me from the walls.

The breakfast room was almost empty except for someone I didn't recognise who was clearing away the last plates from the table. Not a kipper or a piece of buttered toast in sight, and no trace of Ma'am either. That was a bad sign. It could only mean one thing: she was already in her study with a second pot of tea, working through her papers.

Sure enough, that was where I found her. 'Good morning, boy,' she said. 'I saved you a little bit of toast.'

I wagged my tail and nibbled the toast gently from her hand. I was cheered by her reassuring scent that she tips from a tiny glass bottle and dabs behind her ears, that mixture of light flowers and crisp fresh air, heather and kindness. That's the scent I would recognise anywhere, which makes me feel completely at home wherever we are.

After my toast I settled down in the comfy basket under her desk and she returned to her papers. She had a big pile of them that she was picking up one by one, reading intently and scribbling notes on before placing them back in the red box or on a separate pile.

So many papers, every single day. Some of them make her frown, sometimes she sighs, and occasionally they make her eyebrows go right up and then she laughs out loud. We may not go on as many rambling walks as we used to but there are just as many red boxes full of papers as there ever were. She's in her study for hours, which means I'm here, too. In the past I've tried nudging the red box out of her sight to give her more time by the fire with me, but she always notices and says that what needs to be done must be done.

I like it in here. It's cosy and warm with a lovely soft tartan carpet and lots of photographs of all Ma'am's special people arranged on her big desk. It's quiet apart from the crackle of wood in the fire during the winter, and the gentle chiming of the clock on the mantelpiece counting down the hours until tea is served.

Sometimes she will look up from the desk to stare out of the window at the garden and the mountains beyond. That's my cue to stretch up out of my basket and trot with a hopeful look towards the door. But when I try to suggest a walk she smiles and shakes her head and says she's got something to finish. It doesn't seem right to me. No wonder she's so tired. Later we sit together on the pale green sofa. That's my favourite spot in the whole castle. I think it might be hers, too. Sometimes she has tea there by the fire with her guests or her family.

I worry about her. She told me once, not long after I arrived with her, that she hadn't planned to have any more dogs because she didn't want to leave any dog alone *after she'd gone*. That was just before the old Duke left, which made Ma'am so terribly sad. Those were the dark days, when I never left her side for a moment.

Still, today at least, things seem just as they should be. The study is warm and quiet. I can see her feet, crossed at the ankle under her chair, and I can hear her turning papers. I forget to worry, and feel my eyes getting heavier and heavier.

This time I dream of dipping my paws in the cold water of the loch and then racing back to her when she calls me. I am running so fast, skimming over the purple heather, and our walk seems to go on forever, up and over the next Munro towards another and another.

Today was a busy day. Lots of visitors came to see Ma'am so the people were running around all over the place and shouting at me to get out of the way. There were all the usual people with their clipboards and their cups of tea, then some I'd never seen before carrying big vases of flowers, and others in black suits who seemed to be playing hide-and-seek, going in and out of all the rooms and talking into little boxes that made beeping sounds when they held them to their mouths.

It was all too much and I got so frustrated at going unnoticed that I snapped at somebody's ankle as they rushed past. It wasn't even a bite really, just a tiny nip, but I got told off again.

One of the red-coated people took hold of me by my collar and shut me away in the boot room. I was very cross but I didn't want to cause Ma'am any bother on her busy day, so I stayed quiet and bided my time.

None of it mattered in the end because after all the visitors had finally gone, I was let out and called in and she and I sat on the soft, pale green sofa in front of the fire. One of the red-coated people brought in tea and treats, ever so many of them. A cake stand, I think it's called. I remember the time Sandy knocked one over.

I rested my chin in her lap and she gave me some biscuits from the plate on the little square table next to her. I don't like all the things she eats but I do like those crumbly sweet biscuits with the pinpricks in the top, and she kept breaking off more and more for me as she stroked my head and patted my contented tummy.

She hadn't had such a busy day for a long while and though she was tired she seemed happy, too. She had the same feeling about her as I get sometimes, when I've managed to stay close and steer her through a crowd of people, or I've found her an especially good stick and dragged it over. I feel quiet and pleased inside because I know I've done my best and there's nothing more I need to do.

She called to Sandy to sit on the other side of her and though I wished I could have her – and the biscuits – all to myself, I could sense that Sandy was pleased to be there. We watched one another over her lap as she stroked both our heads, and for a moment I felt happier than I have done for a long time.

I didn't see her the next day at all and the people seemed busier and more bothered than ever. I wanted to keep out of the way so I went upstairs to the children's bedrooms. Most of the time nobody goes there except the people with the buckets and mops and the long sticks with the tickly feathers at the end that I love to chew. I crawled under a bed and it was very snug under there.

When the family comes up to stay in the summer, these rooms are cheerful and noisy as the children pull out toys and books to show one another, running in and out of each other's bedrooms. They haven't visited lately but I still remember the game they had last time, when there were delicious chewy feathers raining down from the ceiling as the littlest children swung at each other with pillows.

I got very over-excited – I was only a tiny puppy – and chased the feathers all over the room, under the beds and out into the corridor. We all ended up in a giggling tangled heap and it was only then that I noticed the mess, just at the moment that Ma'am appeared in the doorway.

'Sorry, Great-granny,' I heard the littlest boy say.

She smiled and gave him a hug and me a pat. 'Not to worry,' she said. 'Sometimes games get out of hand. Now, who would like to play charades?'

I do love a big tickly feather. Perhaps I might find one now if I snuffle about in the furthest corners under the bed . . . Nothing.

Those people with their mops must really hate them. There wasn't so much as a speck of dust to be found, never mind a feather.

Eventually I got hungry so I went downstairs to see if there was still a lot of fuss and bother going on, but the whole castle was quiet. Too quiet. It made me nervous.

When I went past the kitchen I saw that our silver food bowls had been filled with something that smelt very tempting. Were we late for supper? How long had I been upstairs under the bed?

I couldn't help wondering why our bowls had been left like this. Usually the people come to find us at mealtimes if we're outside or upstairs. The moment we smell the rich meaty scent of food as it's brought from the castle kitchens, we run to eat. Sometimes, if she has time, Ma'am will serve us herself and we hang back until she has finished spooning chicken and rice or sometimes pheasant or grouse into the bowl. Who had left this food here without calling us? Not her, surely.

I picked at some of the food but I had lost my appetite. I couldn't bear the silence or the sense that Ma'am was in trouble. I had to find her.

Once Sandy had settled down for the night, I crept out and made straight for her bedroom. The hallway was shadowy but her door was open a crack and there was soft light spilling out that made me think she still had her bedside lamp on.

I pushed my nose around the door. There she was, sitting up in bed, her hands resting on the covers. A man in a white coat stood up when he saw me.

'That's all right, let him in,' she said.

One of her hands patted the covers for me to join her. I ran over and jumped onto the bed, turning round and round before I flopped down. But it wasn't like the time before, when she and I had been alone and she had chatted to me quite cheerfully. This time she seemed to be uncomfortable. She stroked me and patted me as usual, but her touch was so light I could hardly feel it.

Then she reached over to the framed photograph on her bedside table and adjusted it slightly. The face she turned to see was the face of the old Duke who was here when I arrived with Ma'am, but who left very soon after. He was a little bit growly with me too, once or twice. Used to get cross when I tried to shepherd her properly from room to room. He was devoted to her, though, I have to admit; as she was to him. I used to get quite jealous because she forgot to pat my tummy or feed me toast whenever he came into the room.

Once she could see his face properly, she closed her eyes.

I knew it was important for her to rest so I settled myself into the chair by her bedside and tried to keep watch over her through the night. I really did try my hardest not to fall asleep, but I can't be certain I managed it because I was half asleep when one of the housemaids scooped me up and took me back to my wicker basket, to spend the rest of the night there.

As she tucked my blanket around me, a fat drop of water fell from her eye and landed on my fur. Then another one. I licked the drops off and tried not to worry. I had done my best. Perhaps Ma'am would be all better in the morning?

When I woke the following day there was a strange heavy feeling in the air. I wondered if there was going to be a thunderstorm, but the weather was fine enough outside in the garden. It was only inside that a dark cloud had settled in, chill and damp. The bustling of the previous days had stopped and we all seemed to be waiting for something. I knew what I was waiting for: to see her. But this time I couldn't stir a muscle to go and look for her. I barely left my basket all day.

The person in the red coat who brought in our breakfast tried to sound cheery when she called us but her voice was shaking. She set out our bowls carefully and I looked up into her face, trying to understand what was wrong.

'Poor little dogs,' she said, stroking our heads in turn. 'You will miss her terribly, won't you? We all will.'

I knew at once who she was talking about, but it simply didn't make any sense. Ma'am never goes anywhere without us; we travel everywhere with her. When she's busy with her papers or at one of her engagements, it's never very long before she comes to find us. Just lately it's been a little harder to track her down but even if I can't find her for a while, I always do in the end.

That's when it hit me. She had gone somewhere I couldn't follow her. She had left for the last time, just as the old Duke had before her. I know what this means. This means that Ma'am is dead. This is why there has been a chill and a heavy silence in the castle. This is why the people have been so strange.

It's too much for me to take in. How can it be true? And if it is true, then all I can think is that I wish I were dead, too.

I don't think I slept at all that night. I wanted her so badly. I kept thinking that she must have wanted me too before she left, and I wasn't with her. This made me so desperately sad.

I paced round the room for hours, listening to Sandy whimper in her sleep. I would resolve to go and find her right away and see if it was really true, then stop in my tracks, knowing it was useless. I could feel that she had gone. I could feel the emptiness growing inside me.

I must have fallen asleep eventually because I opened my eyes to find Sandy licking my face gently and saying, 'Wake up, Muick. We have a visitor.'

It was the nice lady who has been here almost constantly lately; the one who calls Ma'am 'Mummy'. I was so glad to see her that I jumped up and trotted over to sit at her feet and look up into her face. Perhaps there had been a mistake?

But the lady crouched down and explained that Ma'am had passed away, very peacefully. She said that we had brought her so much joy and told us we could always take comfort in our happy memories.

I tried to concentrate on what she was saying but it was as if the words were in some other language I couldn't understand.

The lady was so kind, stroking our fur as she spoke. I could see that she was upset too, even more than we were. I wanted to make her feel better. Ma'am would have wanted me to think of others rather than myself. That was what she always did. So I nuzzled my head into her hand, and for a minute none of us could make any sound at all.

'You'll be going back to Windsor very soon,' the lady said eventually, 'and you will always be well looked after.'

Then she stood up. 'Now, there is a lot to organise. I must get on.'

And with that, she patted us gently one more time and stepped out into the hallway.

Sandy and I looked at each other and bowed our heads. All I could think was that I would never see Ma'am again. Never feel her touch or breathe in her scent or scamper after her out on the hills. There would be no more buttered toast nibbled from her hand, no more siting under her desk or snoozing on the sofa. How would I bear my life without her?

I couldn't stir after the lady left us. I just stayed in my basket.

Sandy went out on little missions to see what was happening and returned with news. 'All her special people are here,' she said as she came back from her first trip. 'They are horribly sad but they're trying to be brave for one another.'

This made my little heart break again, to think of all the people who were suffering. I could hardly stand it.

After her second trip, Sandy returned with the news that the castle was full of people once more. 'They are bringing in letters and packages and ever so many flowers,' she said.

I lifted up my head and asked her, 'Where is Ma'am? Is she still here?'

'I think so,' said Sandy. 'But they won't let me see her.'

I lowered my head back onto my paws. 'In that case I don't want to come out,' I told her.

And I didn't, not for the rest of the day or the day after.

I didn't want to leave the castle when the time came for us to return to Windsor. Once I left Balmoral there would be no way around the fact that she was not with us any more. I felt so lost and alone.

The trip was miserable. Sandy and I sat in our travelling cases next to the people in red coats and black trousers, and nobody said a word the whole way.

Usually I love getting back to Windsor. This is where she and I met when I was still a tiny pup, where she trained me to come when she called and sit when she raised her hand. It's a wonderful old place, and there's always something going on. But how can I enjoy it when she is no longer here? It's impossible. I started to feel so cross that she had gone and left me behind. What was I supposed to do now?

The first day back at Windsor I woke up with a horrible churning feeling in my head and my belly that made me want to run and bark and sink my teeth into something. I didn't know what it was or what to do so I headed out for a walk and found myself making for the old kennels and the stables. I hadn't yet spoken to Emma, Ma'am's favourite pony, but Emma's a wise old thing and I thought perhaps she would be able to help with this nasty feeling that was eating away at me.

All the people in the stables were busy brushing down the horses and polishing the saddles. They seemed sad but determined. None of them looked as if they had a horrible churning in their belly that made

them want to gnash their teeth. This just made me even crosser.

I found Emma standing out in the stable yard, having her mane brushed.

'Muick, you poor thing,' she began. And even though I'd come to talk to her, her kindness made me want to bark my head off. Because Emma was wonderful, but she wasn't *her*. She wasn't Ma'am.

I somehow managed to swallow my barks and looked up at Emma.

'Isn't it terrible?' she continued. 'I've known her all my life; it just doesn't seem possible.'

'What will we do without her? Oh, Emma. I've got the most awful feeling in my belly. I don't know whether to howl or to bite someone.'

'We will do our best,' said Emma. 'We will be kind to one another and to the people, and we will carry on. It's what she would have wanted.'

'You're right,' I said in a small, sad voice. 'I just don't know if I can do it without her.'

Emma nuzzled me with her nose. 'Doing your best means trying every day, even on the bad days. It doesn't mean you have to get it right every time. Remember?'

I nodded and sniffed a little.

'We have each other, and we have the memory of her touch and her laugh and her kind words. We still have her, Muick. Nobody can take away what she gave us.'

Emma was right. It would not be the same without her, but I had not lost everything. I was here because of Ma'am. I was who I was because of her. That would never change, and I would never forget her.

Things have not been quite so bad since my chat with Emma. I miss Ma'am every single minute but I am beginning to feel that I can carry on. Every time I comfort Sandy or potter over to see how Emma is managing, I feel a little bit of Ma'am's strength flow through me. The people are pleased to see me up and about again. It's a comfort to realise that they care about me.

Yesterday, when I was at the stables, I overheard a conversation between two of the people who work there. 'She'll be arriving late in the afternoon,' said one of them. 'She's coming up the Royal Mile on her final journey. I've been asked to take Emma to pay her last respects.'

The other nodded. 'Well, we all want to do that,' he said. 'Have you seen pictures of the Queue? Stretching all along the river. Isn't it magnificent to see how much she was loved and admired?'

I wasn't sure exactly what 'last respects' might be, but I knew immediately that they were talking about Ma'am coming back to Windsor and I resolved that I too would be involved. If there was an opportunity to see her one last time, I must seize it.

Emma explained things to me. Ma'am was lying in state in Westminster . . .

'Lying in what?' I asked.

'In state,' she said firmly, as if she didn't want me to ask any more questions. 'And there will be a gathering in the big church there. For people all over the world to remember her and say their goodbyes.'

I nodded. Emma seemed rather pleased that she knew so much about it.

'And then she will be driven back to Windsor and laid to rest here, next to the old Duke and her mama and papa in the beautiful chapel.'

I nodded again. I knew exactly the place she was talking about. I had been there before with Ma'am, one cold wintery afternoon not so long ago.

She had spent that whole day very quietly, mostly alone. She had signalled me to stay with her straight after breakfast, and I noticed that she was more in the mood for thinking than chatting. Sometimes she liked to tell me about the questions she'd been asked or the matters she'd been pondering but on this particular day she just wanted to sit quietly.

After lunch she called me to her and said, 'We're off to the chapel, Muick. You must be absolutely on your best behaviour, do you understand?'

I gave a little yap to confirm that I did and she nodded. 'Very good. Come along.'

I had never been inside the chapel before. It's extremely grand and rather solemn and there are beautiful windows made of all the colours you can imagine. There are a great many statues and stone carvings, tall wooden seats that look rather uncomfortable, and many flags. I liked it. It felt peaceful.

She sat down on one of the benches and pointed for me to sit at her feet. She bowed her head, closed her eyes and was silent for a little while. Then, when she opened her eyes again, she smiled at me.

'I'm remembering the day I became Queen, Muick. I was such a young girl and though I had tried to prepare myself, it was very hard. My beloved papa was gone. I missed him so much but somehow I had to carry on and do my duty.'

She paused to stroke my head. I stayed very quiet and stared deep into her eyes.

'Well, I learned how to do my job as my papa did before me. I had a lot of help from others, and I've been blessed to do it for a long time. Every year, when the date arrives, I think back to that day. It helps me to prepare for the future. It helps me to feel certain that everything will go on just as it must, Muick.' She scratched my ears. 'We will all go on, just as we must.'

I hadn't thought about that conversation in ages. To be honest, I didn't understand it at the time. I was still little. It's only now, when Emma mentions the chapel, that the memory comes back to me.

If that is where Ma'am will be laid to rest, then I am very pleased. I know it was a place that made her feel peaceful and content, calm and resolute. And she will not be alone there. I won't have to worry about her any more.

That afternoon, I had a lovely visit from some of the children. They are living near the castle now. They had asked their mother if they could come to see us, Sandy and me, and, oh, we were so pleased to have them. Poor things, they looked a bit gloomy. We didn't have it in us to run around or play but we all curled up together on the sofa and that helped a little.

When they were getting up to leave, the little girl said to her mother, 'Will Muick and Sandy be there tomorrow, Mummy?'

'I'm not sure,' she replied. 'We'll have to see.'

I had been thinking about this very thing ever since my conversation with Emma, and as soon as I heard what the little girl said, I went over to her and her mother and did my best-behaved begging face. I wanted them to know how important it was to me to be there. When they looked down at me I gave a tiny bark and wagged my tail hard.

The beautiful lady smiled at me and gave me a pat. I think she understood.

That evening, my favourite of the red-coated people came to give us our supper.

'It's all arranged, Muick,' she said. 'You and Sandy will be brought out onto the steps of the forecourt as Her Majesty's coffin arrives tomorrow. You must promise to be quiet and well behaved. Do you think you can do that?'

Of course I could do that! I bounded over to her and she laughed as I put my paws up on her knees. 'That's all right, boy. I know how much you loved her and what this means to you.'

After she had gone I was too nervous to settle down for the night. There would be a great many people coming to the castle to celebrate Her Majesty's life. The chapel would be full and there would be many more people outside in the park, lining the Royal Mile. The service would be the final opportunity for her family and her close friends to say goodbye, and we must all do our very best to make sure everything went perfectly.

Well, as you can imagine, this made me feel rather anxious. What a lot of responsibility. But as I said to Sandy before we finally closed our eyes, 'It's the least we can do for her and for all her most special people. We shall be the proudest dogs in the whole of England.'

oday is the day of Ma'am's funeral. Today is the day I will say goodbye to her.

I was up bright and early this morning. I was determined to do her proud, to keep my head and remember that the most important thing was to honour her memory and be kind to all those who are missing her.

I also had to set an example to Sandy, just as Ma'am would have wanted. I was rather worried that Sandy might go to pieces, especially when we saw all the crowds and the cameras and the helicopters overhead.

'Gosh,' Sandy said as we looked out of the window. 'There are going to be an awful lot of people looking at us.'

'Not to worry,' I said, trying to sound braver than I felt. 'They will all be there for the same reason that we will – to remember her. They're our friends.'

When the time came I felt quite calm. Two people in red coats and black trousers came and clipped our leads on, and we walked closely at their heels through the great hall and out onto the steps.

There was a hush as we all waited for Ma'am to arrive.

Then, as the bugle sounded, the car bringing her home turned into the courtyard. The fur stood up on my neck and for a moment I thought I would howl.

Then the strangest thing happened. As she was carried past Sandy and me, I looked up. I had been sitting neatly with my head bowed but just then I caught a trace of oak leaves and her pink garden roses, with a hint of rosemary from the palace garden – her favourites. It must have been from the beautiful flowers that were resting on top of the coffin next to her crown. I felt so close to her in that moment. She was gone and yet she was still with me. Sending me a reminder of the love we had shared, just when I needed it the most.

I bowed my head again. 'Thank you, Ma'am, for everything,' I whispered.

I wished her a long, deep rest. She had earned it.

Later on, the little girl came to find me and buried her face in my fur and rubbed my neck. The other children gathered around and we sat together in silence.

Nobody could ever take her place, but with the children's arms around me I could feel her love, still flowing through them and through me. I will always be her dog, but now I am theirs as well.

And far away, in some corner of my mind, I heard her say, 'That's the spirit, Muick . . . That's the spirit.'

Windsor Castle

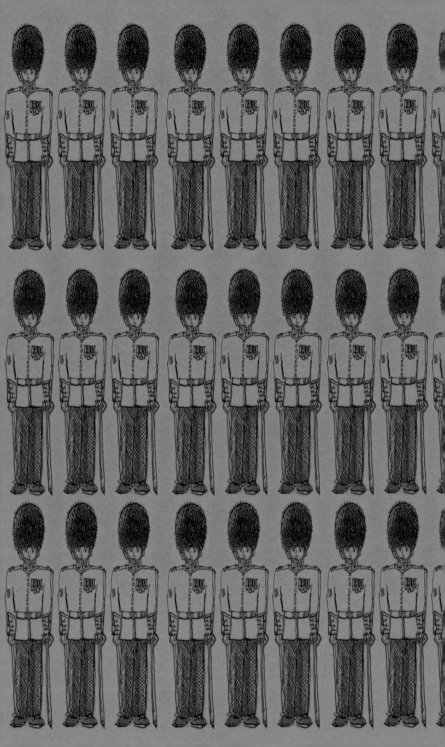